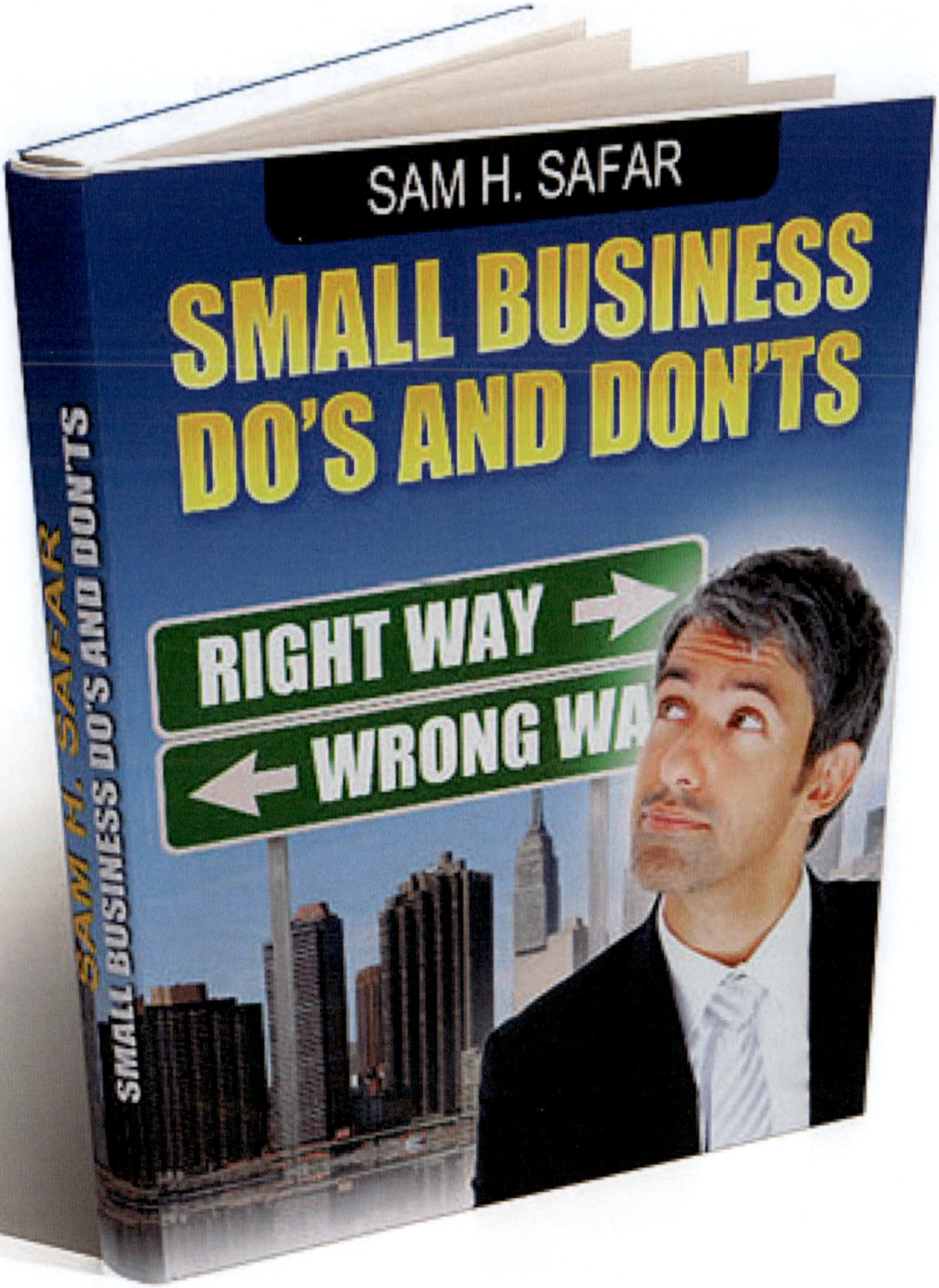
SAM H. SAFAR
SMALL BUSINESS
DO'S AND DON'TS
RIGHT WAY
WRONG WA
SAM H. SAFAR
SMALL BUSINESS DO'S AND DON'TS

Small Business

Do's and Don'ts

Volume I

Publisher: zYouSoft, Inc.
Http://www.zYouSoft.com

ISBN: 978-0-9832335-0-3

Sam H. Safar

Sam H. Safar, author, poet and inventor; came to the United States searching for his dream. Mr. Safar lived in the Midwest for fifteen years before moving to the West Coast. He now lives with his wife and five children in San Diego, California. Mr. Safar's inspiration to write for business comes from the busy and special time he spends daily on his small business. Mr. Safar received a B.S. Degree from University of Minnesota.

Most of Mr. Safar's writing focus is around small business, entrepreneurs and their dreams. He shares in their ambitions. He also developed Patent-Pending "**Player Performance Level**" (PPL) scoring system that standardizes measuring athletes ranking. **Http://www.pplsorts.com/**

The Small Business Do's and Don'ts are some of the most creative, imaginative, and creative books available for young entrepreneurs today.

The YELLOW PIG stories are some of the most creative, imaginative, and funny books available for young children today.

Publisher: zYouSoft, Inc.
Http://www.zYouSoft.com

ISBN: 978-0-9832335-0-3

TABLE OF CONTENTS

The Start-Up

1. DO Think Big! 2
2. DO Be Positive 4
3. DON'T Associate With Negative People 6
4. DO Get Into A Business You'll Enjoy....7
5. DON'T Get Into A Business You Know Nothing About 9
6. DON'T Start From Scratch....10
7. DO Buy an Established Business....11
8. DON'T Buy a Business That's in the Red....12
9. DON'T Join A Franchise....14
10. DON'T Choose a Retail Business If You Don't Like Dealing With People....15
11. DO Believe In Your Product....17
12. DO Have a Short-Term and a Long-Term Business Plan....18
13. DO Secure Your Idea....19
14. DO Incorporate 21
15. DON'T Invest Your Own Money 22
16. DON'T Borrow From Relatives 24
17. DO Obtain Working Capital....26
18. DON'T Buy Expensive Equipment 27
19. DON'T Buy Used Merchandise From People You Don't Trust....28
20. DON'T Sign Expensive Leases 29
21. DON'T Sign Long-Term Leases....30
22. DO Pay COD When You Start 31
23. DO Create a Strong Color Logo....33
24. Notes 35

Conducting Business

25. DO Pay Attention to Your Appearance 37
26. DON'T Become A Cheap Employee at Your Own Business 38
27. DO Stay Healthy: Physically and Mentally 40
28. DON'T Hire Relatives or Close Friends 41
29. DO Hire People With Nice Smiles 42
30. DO Hire Good-Looking People 43
31. DO Hire People Smarter Than You 44
32. DO Hire Outside Sales People 45
33. DO offer Incentives To Boost Morale and Increase Productivity 46
34. DO Listen To Your Employees' Advice 47
35. DO Advertise 48
36. DO Hold Sales and Annual Promotions 49
37. DON'T Manufacture Your Product until You Sell It 51
38. DON'T Sell Below Cost 53
39. DO Keep Your Eye on Expenses 54
40. DON'T Spend Your Money Lavishly 55
41. DO Pay Your Taxes and Keep Good Records 56
42. Notes 58

The Customer

43. DO Know Your Customers 60
44. DO Flatter Your Customers 62
45. DO Listen, Listen, Listen 63
46. DO Know What Your Customers Expect 64
47. DO Make Customer Satisfaction Your Number One Priority 66

The Customer (cont.)

48. DO Deliver More Than Customers Expect 68
49. DO Deliver On-Time Service 69
50. DO Aim for Quick Service 71
51. DO Accept Checks 73
52. DO Accept Credit Cards 74
53. DO Keep Your Eye on Your Money 75
54. DON'T Extend Credit To Small Customers 76
55. Notes 77

Time to Sell?

56. DON'T Be Afraid of Goliath 79
57. DO Plan For Goliath 81
58. DO Know When to Fold 83
59. DO Sell When You Get an Offer 84
60. Notes 85

Summary

The Do's and Don'ts of Doing Business 87

"Recovering from failure is often easier than building from success."

Michael D. Eisner

THE DO'S AND DON'TS OF STARTING YOUR NEW BUSINESS

DO Think Big!

"If you want to be a big company tomorrow, you have to start acting like one today."

Thomas J. Watson, Jr., IBM

No matter what business you're in, you must *think big* to achieve more. If you don't think big, your small business will remain just that—small. Ask yourself what your goals are both for your business and for your personal finances. Once you've determined your goals, devise a plan for achieving them. The key to success is to develop a business plan that offers your customers something none of your existing or future competitors offer them. If you can do that, you needn't worry about the industry giants moving into your territory, because someday you *will be that giant!*

CASE IN POINT

I would describe the copy business I opened in California as very professional, both in its appearance and operation. Many of my customers asked if the store was a franchise and were surprised to learn that it was not. Satisfied with my customer base and my profits, I never planned for expansion. I told myself the hassle wasn't worth it. Can you guess what happened? When Mr. Big in the office supply world (Staples) opened a store a half mile from mine, I was unprepared. Without a plan for expansion, I couldn't compete. In less than one year, I closed my copy shop. In the meantime, *Mail Boxes, Etc* and *Sir Speedy Printing Centers* survived because they not only had big dreams, they had well-thought-out plans for making their dreams a reality.... step by step.

LESSON

If you want to last more than five years, you must think big, know your goals, and have a plan for reaching them.

Tip #1

Believe and you WILL achieve!

YOU CAN USE THIS SPACE TO:

Note your goals and plans.

DO Be Positive

"I am an optimist. It does not seem too much use being anything else."

Michel de Montaigne

Attitude, attitude, attitude! The key to success in business is your inner "self-talk". If you are planning to launch a business, or for that matter any project in life, you must realize that not everything will go smoothly or according to plan. If a door slams in your face, you must believe another door will open *and you must look for it.* Do not give up! Maintain a positive attitude! When I launch a company, I tell myself that I will persevere, that I will try new strategies, that if one strategy doesn't work, I will try another. If problems arise—and they inevitably do—I open my mind to a variety of solutions. If you keep trying to solve a problem, you will solve it!

Between problems at work, at home, with children, with money, everyone feels discouraged at times—but true entrepreneurs never give up. My goal is big money and my attitude is: I will not abandon my goal, I will achieve it! If you are in business and feel like giving up, change your attitude. Find new ways to do things, new ways to make money. If you just sit there waiting for your business to improve by itself, you are waiting for disaster.

CASE IN POINT

My husband didn't like his business. He derived virtually no enjoyment at all from his work and no longer believed it worth the effort. After months of discouragement and depression, he decided to work for someone else. As soon as he did that he was far happier. He wasn't a true entrepreneur. If you can't tolerate the problems that come with every new venture, if you aren't willing to try to solve these problems, you are better off working for somebody else.

LESSON

If you don't believe your business will be successful, no one else will either!

<u>Tip #2</u>

Keep a positive attitude.

YOU CAN USE THIS SPACE TO:

Write examples of self-talk that help you feel like an entrepreneur.

DON'T Associate With Negative People

"Your attitude, not your aptitude, will determine your altitude."

Zig Ziglar

Starting a business requires gigantic quantities of positive energy and this positive energy must come from within you. Associating with negative people will suck the energy right out of you. It is that simple. You are ready to start a business when you are excited and energized by an idea you want to pursue. It's natural to want to share your excitement, but take care who you share it with. Ninety percent of the population will tell you why your idea **won't** work. The majority of the population consists of followers who crave security and avoid taking risks. They may even feel threatened by or jealous of creative people who have big dreams and the guts to follow through on them. As an entrepreneur, it's imperative that you be aware of this. When your idea is in its infant stage, STAY AWAY from negative people. As *Nike* advertises, "Just Do It!" Don't give nay-sayers the opportunity to deflate your dreams.

CASE IN POINT

I love my husband dearly and want to spend the rest of my life with him. However, he's a person who clings to routine and craves security. The last thing I need is to come home and discuss the day's problems with him. He can't give me words of encouragement because he focuses on the possibility of failure not the prospect of success. Instead, I listen to my positive self-talk for the energy and excitement to continue on toward my goals.

LESSON

Success breeds success.

Tip #3

Join entrepreneur clubs to associate with like-minded, positive-thinking people!

DO Get into a Business You'll Enjoy

"To love what you do and feel that it matters, how could anything be more fun."

Katharine Graham, Washington Post

Another major key to success is to start a business you *love.* Then the work of running the business bestows happiness not headaches! Most rewarding of all, perhaps, is the much-loved hobby that you turn into a successful business. If you truly enjoy and love what you do, you won't even view it as work, but as pure enjoyment and the long hours you devote to building your business will feel like a pleasure, not a necessary evil.

Your long-term success depends on how much you enjoy what you do. If you're in it strictly for the money...sad case! You won't be happy and you will not succeed as quickly or as easily as if you pursue something you enjoy.

CASE IN POINT

My brother was an excellent dentist who knew how to interact well with his patients. They trusted him and continued to return to him for treatment year after year. However, there came a time when he no longer enjoyed his practice because he disliked the petty confrontations that sometimes occurred among his office staff and he abhorred the necessity to give time and attention to the management aspects of running a practice, which is, after all, a small business. Because of the impact his lack of enthusiasm had on the atmosphere at the office, productivity declined and the business suffered financially. What a pity that after so many years of education, after paying off the student loans he accumulated, he had so little joy in his profession.

LESSON

It is important that you love what you do so you will have the enthusiasm and energy to care for the day-to-day operations of the business.

Tip #4

Do what you love....
the money will follow!

YOU CAN USE THIS SPACE TO:

Note the kinds of businesses you think you'd enjoy.

DON'T Get Into a Business You Know Nothing About

"The less you know how to do your work the harder it is to do it."
Henry L. Doherty

Your overall understanding of the business you chose to run is another key to success or failure. You must understand the product, service, or manufacturing process before you undertake the business. Educate yourself about every aspect of the business including the day-to-day operations. You do not want to have to rely totally on the people you hire for information. The bottom line is that it's <u>your</u> business. No matter how hard an employee works or how much knowledge that person brings to your business, he or she will never invest the energy, love, or sweat it will take to make the business a success the way you will. It's your baby, not theirs.

CASE IN POINT

When I opened my pizza restaurant, I knew nothing about running a restaurant. I thought I'd just hire people with experience and rely on their expertise. I found out that this is a very expensive way to start a business, certainly not appropriate for someone with a limited budget. It took me over a year to sufficiently understand the business and what the customers expected so that I could make a profit.

LESSON

One important step in setting up a successful business is choosing a business you know about.

<u>Tip #5</u>

Know your business!

DON'T Start From Scratch

"They who know how to employ opportunities will often find that they can create them."
John Stuart Mill

Oh, it is so painful to change your thinking habits. If you believe you must start your new business from scratch, not starting from scratch is such a hard concept to entertain. The start-up of a new business is a challenge and all true entrepreneurs love a challenge. But you don't need to start a business from scratch to experience a challenge. Can you imagine taking over a business that has already gone through its growing pains and, now that the kinks are worked out, building on it to make it even more successful? If you doubt this, just think of some of the *Microsoft* products! Starting a new business from scratch can be lonely and scary. If you've tried and failed, don't let that fear paralyze you. Try again by building on someone else's beginnings.

CASE IN POINT

When I invented something I thought other people might benefit from, I started a business from scratch to produce it. I thought if I maintained control of all aspects of the business, I could keep all the profits. I didn't want anyone else to reap rewards from my idea. I did the purchasing, set up the tools, took the orders and filled them—everything myself from scratch. Did I keep all the profits this way? Of course NOT! Since I had to buy the raw materials, suppliers profited from my invention. Was the quality of the product better because I did it all myself? Of course NOT! I was overworked and the quality of my product suffered as I tried to meet deadlines. Did I learn I couldn't do it all myself? You bet I did.

LESSON

You are in business to make money, not work yourself to death!

Tip #6
Don't reinvent the wheel!

DO Buy an Established Business

"There are always opportunities through which business can profit if they will only recognize and seize them."

J. Paul Getty

If you are not starting something completely and uniquely new, then save your soul, your capital, and your sanity. Buy an established business. If you want to open a dry cleaning business or a pizza restaurant, see if any are for sale in your area. Save yourself the headache of having to find a building, equipment, employees, etc. Follow the Do's and Don'ts in this manual when you look for a business to buy. Choose a business you're interested in and know something about, one that's been successful in the past and you can visualize growing. Research your market. Then buy *only* what you can afford!

CASE IN POINT

You might think that if a business is for sale, it must be a loser. This is not true. There are many reasons why businesses are for sale. People get ill, retire, and want to relocate, or just burn out. Look in your local newspaper or business journal, or contact a business broker to obtain a listing of businesses for sale near you. If you have the money to launch a business, you're wiser to invest it in an existing business that has a successful track record. Your investment will not be nearly as risky and you'll see a return on your investment sooner. It can take a brand new business several months or years to see a profit. In general, when you buy an existing business, you get to do what you like best, and you make money faster.

LESSON

Buy an existing business to get a quicker return on your investment!

<u>Tip #7</u>

Buy a business on its way up...not down!

DON'T Buy a Business That's in the Red

"Luck is a matter of preparation meeting opportunity."

Oprah Winfrey

You've decided you don't want to start from scratch; you've called a business broker and/or looked in the paper for a business for sale. You're on the right track. Just remember this: People sell their business for a reason and you MUST know what that reason is. Ask the seller directly. Check the accounting books and bank statements. Talk with the employees. Work in the business for a month so you can be there and take notes. Study the business for at least *sixty* days and make certain the reason for the sale is not that the business is in the RED (losing money).

As you study the business, do your own investigative work. You can ask your accountant to help you, but don't depend 100 percent on this person. It is you, not your accountant or broker, who is investing the money and you who has something to lose. Therefore, it is you who must make this decision. If you are considering buying a company in the RED because it's cheap and you believe you can turn it around and make a profit, you must be out of your mind! Run; don't walk, away from it! There are plenty of sound businesses (in the black) out there that are being sold due to the owner's poor health, retirement, divorce, lack of enthusiasm, or relocation. You don't need to start with a loser.

CASE IN POINT

A friend of mine owns a small grocery store in an unexciting area of the city. I asked him one day if he would sell his business. He replied, "Why? I'm making good money." Business owners who are making money, enjoying the business, and are in good health, will hang on to their businesses unless they have a compelling reason not to. A good business is its owner's golden egg. Keep looking until you find an owner who is making money but has a legitimate personal reason to sell.

Lesson

Know what you're buying before you hand out the cash.

Tip #8

Do your own homework. Don't trust your broker 100 percent.

YOU CAN USE THIS SPACE TO:

Note information about a business you are investigating.

DON'T Join a Franchise

"Free enterprise will work if you will."

Ray Kroc

Franchising has been called the true American mall builder. If you have money to invest and are interested in the retail or service sector, buying into a franchise *can* be one way, but frankly, it is not my favorite way. And if you consider it, you MUST be careful! Don't buy into a franchising company without doing your homework. There are deceptive franchisers out there who are only after the quick buck. Find out what the return will be on your investment and for how long you will get it. Learn how much support you can count on from the franchiser and what protection you will receive. Study how other franchisees are doing and how much free rein they are allowed. A franchisee is *not* an entrepreneur. A franchisee reports to the franchiser who dictates certain expenditures, for example, what you spend on advertising. As a franchisee, you will work long hard hours, and you will then hand over some of your profits to the franchiser. Find out how much you will keep.

CASE IN POINT

Not too long ago I spoke with a submarine sandwich shop franchisee. He informed me that after everybody, meaning the franchiser, the suppliers, etc., took their cut, he ended up with one-eighth of the sub sandwich sales price. He was complaining that his profit was not worth the effort. He could have invested in a non-franchise business and for his hard work made more money with a lot less headache.

LESSON

Don't pay someone else a big share for your hard work.

Tip #9

Read the find print.

DON'T Choose a Retail Business if You Don't Like Dealing with People

"If you don't genuinely like your customers, the chances are they won't buy."
Thomas J. Watson, Jr., IBM

Retail sales is the most difficult type of business an entrepreneur can undertake and it isn't for everyone. A retailer must be a true risk taker, and since the retailer interacts directly with the public, he or she *must* be a people person who enjoys constant contact with a variety of people. The most successful retailers are those individuals who have no problem striking up conversations with complete strangers, who take rejection well, and who thrive in a busy, confusing environment. The retailer needs a special personality—that of a sales person who actually prefers to be surrounded by people most of the time.

CASE IN POINT

Studies designed to determine why some people excel in one type of business rather than another have found that the most successful retail owners possess the following characteristics and skills:

- Ability to establish and maintain warm and genuine interpersonal relationships with others (customers),
- Sincere desire to improve another person's quality of life (customer satisfaction),
- Ability to learn and master skills before using them (knowing their business thoroughly),
- Ability to work with many people to reach a harmonious goal (little or no conflict) while maintaining control,
- Ability to use effective procedures and make decisions,
- Ability to organize the work of those around them to ensure that things run smoothly and efficiently.

If this describes you, then a retail business may be for you.

LESSON

Use your special talents to make the most of your business.

Tip #10

Stay out of retail... UNLESS you have a "retail personality"!

YOU CAN USE THIS SPACE TO:

List the characteristics you have that would make you a successful retailer.

DO Believe in Your Product

"A mediocre idea that generates enthusiasm will go further than a great idea that inspires no one."

Mary Kay Ash (Mary Kay Cosmetics)

I've created a few inventions and have spent considerable sums of money developing them, but with some of my inventions, I stopped at a prototype. I continued other inventions through to production, although most of my inventions failed to become successful products. When I analyzed the reasons for this, I realized that the failure was due to one factor: I didn't believe sufficiently in my product. As an entrepreneur, I've learned that you can't sell a product unless you truly believe in it.

CASE IN POINT

I love inventing, but that wasn't enough for success. Even though most of my friends and acquaintances thought my inventions were great ideas, I didn't believe in them enough to work hard on marketing them. After a few months of marketing my products, I'd stop. You must believe whole-heartedly in your product in order to convince people to buy it. If you believe in it, you can describe its advantages with enthusiasm and convince people it is something they want to own.

LESSON

Make sure your product is one you'll continue to believe in long after its creation.

TIP #11

Necessity is the Mother of Invention!

DO Have a Short-Term and a Long-Term Business Plan

"People who fail to plan, have planned to fail."
George Hewell

Having a plan, both a short and a long term business plan, whether professionally prepared or prepared on a restaurant napkin, gives you confidence and turns a nebulous idea into a concrete goal. Whether you are inventing a new product, marketing a new product, or buying an existing business, your primary objective is to make money. When significant problems arise, go back to your plan, and if you're a true entrepreneur, you will say, "Aha! This is where I need to make an adjustment." A good business plan that includes both short and long-term goals helps you to stay on course. There are no guarantees, of course, but when your venture is successful, at least you will know why. And you will have a blueprint for future ventures. Plus, it's fun to say to your peers, "See, I planned this whole operation...on a restaurant napkin!"

CASE IN POINT

Whether I'm relaxing on my recliner (it's worth noting that my recliner's comfortable leather gets softer as I get older) or energetically pursuing my dreams, the comfort I derive from having a business plan that keeps me on track towards my goal is invaluable.

LESSON

If you have a clear idea of where you're going, you won't get lost. It is easy to get off track.

<u>Tip #12</u>

Plan your work.
Work your plan.

DO Secure Your Idea

"I dream for a living."
Steven Spielberg

Whether what you have in your head is an idea for a business, a book, or a new invention, you must secure your idea. New and unique ideas that earn serious money are very hard to come by. On the other hand, how many times have you seen products in the stores and said to yourself, "I thought of that ten years ago?" Ideas are what make us human, make our businesses prosper and make us money. But you must establish ownership of your idea if you hope to profit by it. If you have an idea and are a serious businessperson, the first thing I suggest you do is register your idea. Do you know that the person who invented the ballpoint pen never patented it and never made a penny off of it?

CASE IN POINT

There are many ways to register your idea. One is to contact the Patent Office at the Register of Copyrights at the Library of Congress in Washington, DC. You can request free information about filing a patent and registering your idea by calling 1-202-287-9100. However, acquiring a patent can be an expensive and long, drawn-out process, running into thousands of dollars.

An alternative, less expensive way to secure ideas that I use is this: When I get a new idea, I write it down or illustrate it, then I have one or two people I know <u>well</u> sign their names as witnesses and date the signature. I then mail this to myself, by <u>registered</u> mail. I never open the envelope after that. You never now when you'll need to open it in front of a judge. In my opinion, ideas are as good as the money they produce for you. Just ask my husband, who always says, "if it's such a great idea, how come you're not making money from it?"

LESSON

We all have great ideas every now and then. It's only those few who claim and act upon their ideas who achieve success.

Tip #13

Register your ideas
before someone else has the same idea ...
and becomes a millionaire!

YOU CAN USE THIS SPACE TO:

Note your ideas.

DO Incorporate

"A man to carry on a successful business must have imagination. He must see things as in a vision, a dream of the whole thing."

Charles Schwab

Because you took the risk of buying this manual, I know that you have the soul of an entrepreneur and I expect that you will be starting your own business. Before you sign any contract or lease or borrow money, do one thing: INCORPORATE. This will afford you invaluable protection if you are a victim of life's unpredictable ups and downs. If you are the least bit legally savvy, you could purchase an "incorporation kit" from an office supply store. These kits include forms and step-by-step instructions for incorporating. The kit costs between twenty-five and seventy-five dollars. In addition, there are fees of roughly seventy-five dollars for filing the forms at the courthouse. It's an easy procedure if you feel confident doing it yourself. If not, it is worth the extra money now to hire an attorney and do it right.

CASE IN POINT

Before I opened my copy business, my former accountant advised me to incorporate. You know what I did? I fired her! Two years later, I had to file bankruptcy and I lost much more than the attorney's fees. I should have listened to her to begin with.

Special Note: Should your company ever be sued, should your business fail, should you be ordered to pay damages, should there not be enough funds, should your company be forced to file bankruptcy, the other parties can NOT come after your personal property *if* you are incorporated. On the other hand, if you are NOT incorporated, you can lose everything: your business, your home, your car, even your purebred dog!

LESSON

Whether you hire an attorney or do it yourself, you must incorporate!

Tip #14

Incorporate, incorporate, incorporate.
Did I say that enough? Okay, INCORPORATE!

Don't Invest Your Own Money

"I have enough money to last me the rest my life, unless I buy something"
Jackie Mason

Anyone who is inclined to lend you money wants to see you invest some of your own money in the business as well, unless, of course, you're Donald Trump. Most of the time it is exceedingly difficult to secure a loan, but if you can arrange for a loan, without resorting to loan sharks, do it. Legitimate sources of loans include banks, credit unions, and small business loans from the government. Borrowing money to start or improve a business is, in my opinion, the best way of doing business. If you've financed your business venture with borrowed money and the business does not succeed, you'll keep your house, you won't be flat broke, and your spouse may still be happy with you. You'll sleep better knowing you have preserved some liquid assets (cash) somewhere.

NOTE: See Section 14 (Incorporating) and Section 16 (Money From Relatives)

CASE IN POINT

When your business is not realizing the income you hoped, you might think it would be easier to walk to your bank and withdraw money from your account than suffer the pain of trying to borrow money from a financial institution. In the short run, it might indeed be easier, but in the long run, it isn't, and because once your money is gone you will find it a great deal harder to obtain a loan. You see, if you don't have cash, lenders have no collateral, no insurance for the loan. You need money to borrow money. This is a Catch 22 I often remind my banker of. She throws back her head, laughs, then replies, "We are in the business of making money, too!"

LESSON

It takes money to make money, but borrow the money rather than spend your own..before yours is all gone!

Tip #15

Keep your money in the bank!

YOU CAN USE THIS SPACE TO:

Note names, addresses, and phone numbers of legitimate sources of loans in your area.

DON'T Borrow From Relatives

"Wisdom consists in being able to distinguish among dangers and make a choice of the least harmful."

Niccolo Machiavelli

Whether you are already in business or are about to start a business, you have to learn the do's and don'ts of borrowing money. Borrowing money is essential for business. One bit of conventional wisdom most business advisers will give you is to avoid borrowing money from your friends and relatives. It seems natural to think that your relatives would be more lenient with loan repayments because their collection systems are not formal. But for this very reason, it might be too easy for you to put off repaying them or you might put so much pressure on yourself to pay them back that you end up causing yourself what I call " Relative Money Stress Syndrome." Moreover, your relatives might be less lenient than you think about the terms of payment. Very likely, your relationship with the friends and relatives from whom you've borrowed money will be strained until you have fully repaid your loan.

CASE IN POINT

I once borrowed five thousand dollars from my brother to meet my payroll. Every time I bumped into him, I worried that he would ask for the money I owed him. Finally, to escape this pressure, I decided to write him two checks, each for twenty-five hundred dollars. One check was to be cashed right away, but I asked him to hold the other until I had enough money in the bank to cover it. Well, guess what? After just two weeks, he called and wanted to know when he could cash the second check! I knew very well that he had enough money, but he made me feel like I was going to cheat him. I tried very hard that week to save enough money to pay him back. And believe me, when I did, I felt as if an elephant had been lifted off my back!

Special Note: Some lenders will ask you to guarantee some loans with personal assets (collateral). If at all possible, don't do this. Try instead for a signature loan. Other avenues to pursue include: (1) Small Business Loans, (2) Government Grants, and (3) New Business Incubator Projects. Contact your local Small Business Administration office for details.

Lesson

Borrow money from outsiders. The stresses of borrowing from family members are not worth it.

Tip #16

Don't borrow money from your relatives ...or from your friends!

DO Obtain Working Capital

"You hit home runs not by chance, but by preparation."

Roger Maris

Working capital is the money available to you after you take care of your start-up expenses. Working capital will provide funds for your payroll, utilities, telephone, and so on. If you spend all your money on start-up, you will have no money to see your business through until the day it starts to earn a profit. Don't expect to make money the minute you start your business. At first, you will likely have more expenses than income. Some businesses require at least six to nine months of working capital. You must accurately estimate the working capital you'll need and your business plan should help you do this. (Lending institutions will require a complete business plan when you request a loan.) In my opinion, working capital is like rain in a dry season.

NOTE: See Sections 12 (Plans), 15 (Own Money), and 16 (Relatives).

CASE IN POINT

There's nothing more discouraging than finally getting your business set up, only to find you have to borrow funds to complete your first job. This creates a vicious cycle that, once started, is very difficult, if not impossible, to break. This situation alone is responsible for most business failures in the first year.

LESSON

Adjust your spending of working capital as your business begins to have income that matches its expenses.

<u>Tip #17</u>

Borrow enough money so you have the working capital to keep your business going until you have a good cash flow!

DON'T Buy Expensive Equipment

"You can have it all, you just can't have it all at once."

Oprah Winfrey

If the business you're starting needs equipment or furniture, shop around first. Deal with reputable vendors, obtain references from business associates, pay attention to warranties, and compare prices. Beware! You get what you pay for. Don't buy items that are so cheap they won't meet your needs, but don't buy a Cadillac when a Vega (Do they still make those?) will do. You can always trade up later when your cash flow has been established. You must use your working capital wisely when starting your business.

CASE IN POINT

I got a call from my accountant one day to ask what I paid for the small copiers in my shop. As if he didn't know—he had all my financial records. But instead, he called me to describe the copier he'd just bought at an auction for four hundred dollars. My accountant just had to rub it in. You see, I'd just bought some new six thousand dollar copiers only to have them break down repeatedly during the first four months my copy shop was in business. The service technician kept informing me that all new copiers need adjustment the first few months. That's not exactly what a small business owner wants to hear--especially when he's just opened a new copy shop that depends on the copiers running non-stop without glitches!

LESSON

Shop around and buy good, but reasonably priced, merchandise. It is your money, after all.

Tip #18

Spend wisely or not at all.

DON'T Buy Used Merchandise from People You Don't Trust

"Things are seldom what they seem. Skim milk masquerades as cream."
William Gilbert

Trust. What is trust in business? After a bad experience with a secondhand purchase, I believed that all people were sharks, that as long as they made a buck, they didn't care what they did to me. I *learned* to be distrustful. I learned the hard way to be careful with whom and from whom I purchased the items I needed for my business. Secondhand purchases can work if you obtain some kind of warranty, but the warranty *must be backed by solid support.* Be careful: Do your homework, check out the company, check the address (never accept a P.O. Box as an address), drive by the company, ask for names of other satisfied customers...and call them!

CASE IN POINT

I purchased a used folding machine from a man claiming to be a dealer specifically for that kind of machine. When I made that purchase, I ignored my gut instincts and the advice of my staff. I fell for what I thought was a great deal. The vendor gave me a paper he claimed was a ninety-day warranty from his company. After just a few uses, I had problems with the machine. I called the vendor. He didn't return my calls. His address was a P.O. Box.

You can fill in the blanks of the story from that point on. I was fooled by a con man. Be careful!

LESSON

It is better to deal with a reputable company that backs up its products, even if you have to pay more. Don't be cheap; be smart!

<u>Tip #19</u>

If you trust your gut instincts, you will seldom go wrong!

DON'T Sign Expensive Leases

"Every morning, I get up and look through the 'Forbes' list of the richest people in America. If I'm not there, I go to work."

Robert Orben, Writer

If you're in business as long as I've been in business, sooner or later you'll probably sign a lease, either for office space, equipment rental, a car, whatever. When you sign a lease, keep your business plan in mind. If you're not on the 'Forbes' list of the richest people in America, and my guess is you're not there yet, don't overextend yourself and don't assume things will always go well in the future. Be logical and practical when you choose an office. Do not get carried away, no matter how beautiful it is. What's important is not how beautiful the office is, but how beautiful the deal is that you make for it. It's your business plan and your cash flow that will impress investors, not an office with a window overlooking the ocean.

NOTE: See Section 12 (Business Plans)

CASE IN POINT

A business person who signs an expensive lease is like a beautiful bride who spends a fortune on her wedding, thinking her handsome husband is worth every cent of it, without considering that in a few months he might run away with a richer, or younger, or more beautiful, woman. Agree only to what you can afford and watch out for those convincing sales people!

LESSON

Don't overextend yourself! A lease is a legal document and you are obligated by its terms.

<u>Tip #20</u>

Make due with what you CAN afford!

DON'T Sign Long-Term Leases

"Any game you play, you got to lose sometime."
Roy Acuff

Again, be careful here. Sometimes, long-term leases appear attractive because of a lower monthly payment and/or the freebies you're promised for signing the long-term lease. Unless you have solid long-term financial backing for your business, avoid this devil. Sign a long-term lease *only after* your business is well established. A long-term lease looks good on the leasing company's financial statement. The leasing company saves expenses by signing you to a long-term lease, but it may not be the best option for you.

CASE IN POINT

In the course of doing businesses, I once had the option of signing a five-year lease with the first three months free and a reduction in the monthly rent or signing a month-to-month lease with a higher monthly rent. I was so confident that my business would succeed no matter what--*which is NOT an attitude you need to take when dealing with legal contracts*--that I signed the longer lease. After only one year, the economy hit a slump (Can I blame President Carter?) and my business was one of the thousands of victims. Nonetheless, I had to honor the terms of the lease because the landlord refused to renegotiate. I suffered a huge loss. The wise move would have been to start cautiously, monitor the progress of my business, and enter renegotiations with the landlord when the business was on solid ground—another lesson I learned the hard way.

LESSON

Everything is negotiable except health and death.

<u>Tip #21</u>

Start with a month-to-month lease.

DO Pay COD When You Start

"What can be added to the happiness of a man who is in health, out of debt? and has a clear conscience?"

Adam Smith

This advice is essential if you are not incorporated, but even if you are, I believe it's a good idea to pay Cash On Delivery (COD) when you start your new business. Some business people may disagree with me on this, but, in my opinion, "net thirty" is the equivalent of charging the item. I recommend a COD policy for your purchases *for at least the first three months* after you start your business. Because cash walks out the door faster than you can imagine, paying COD is the only way to truly get an accurate feeling for your cash flow. It allows you to keep a true focus on your spending so that you will not overextend yourself during the first few months in business. That is the last thing you want to do because, once you get in the hole, you may never be able to climb out of it.

CASE IN POINT

Countless numbers of people pay for their household purchases, even food, by credit card. They pay the minimum monthly balance due on the bill, and eventually they are so deep in debt, they have to declare bankruptcy. The same concept applies to your business expenses. I am grateful to the vendors who demand Cash On Delivery from me. These vendors understand that when you purchase merchandise without paying for it immediately, you are essentially charging it, and when charging purchases, it is very easy to lose track of how much you spend. Then, when the bill arrives, you are tempted to pay the "minimum balance due," and the next thing you know, all of your payments are going toward interest and your principle barely decreases. Moreover, if your business doesn't do well, you might end up with collections agencies on your back.

LESSON

Cash accounting is a simple accounting method that gives a truer feeling of the performance of a new business and its cash flow during the first few months of operation.

Tip #22

Cash--now you see it, now you don't.

YOU CAN USE THIS SPACE TO:

Review the reasons for paying COD during the start-up phase of a business.

DO Create a Strong Color Logo

"Making the simple complicated is commonplace; making the complicated simple, awesomely simple, that's creativity."

Charles Mingus

Image is *very* important. A logo represents your business, and by extension a logo represents you personally. The colors, the design, the message—all of these convey an impression of your business. Make sure your logo conveys the image you want it to. A professional can help you decide upon and design a logo for your company. If you design a logo yourself, ask other people their opinions of your logo and listen carefully to their feedback. What do they think? What image are they getting? What suggestions or ideas can they offer? Your logo will define your business, possibly forever. It should be more than just a pretty design; it should express a thought and a message.

CASE IN POINT

Look at an egg. An egg sends an immediate message: nourishment, productivity, simplicity, and a miracle. You could not design a better image than an egg for this message. The same should be true of a logo. It must perfectly express the message you want your company to send. I believe that logos should be simple in design, but unique. Consider the most familiar logos, such as those for *Nike*, *IBM*, or *Exxon*. They are very simple logos, yet people recognize them instantly. Simplicity is the rule, but there can be exceptions. *Microsoft*'s logo, for example, is complex; it expresses a complicated technology.

LESSON

It's definitely worth time, effort, and even some money, to develop strong logo for your company.

Tip #23

A logo is your company's signature.
Make it simple, yet eye-catching!

YOU CAN USE THIS SPACE TO:

Make notes or sketch ideas for your logo.

Section Notes:

"Good Fortune is what happens when opportunity meets with preparation."

Thomas Edison

THE DO'S AND DON'TS OF CONDUCTING BUSINESS

DO Pay Attention to Your Appearance

"More often than not, things and people are as they appear."

Malcolm Forbes

Fair or not, your customers and clients base their first impression of you and your business on your appearance. Therefore, before you start your day, look in a full-length mirror. Be sure your clothes are clean and fit well, your hair is neat, and the image you present is the image you want to present. To succeed in business, you need to look sharp. Personal hygiene is also very important as is not overdoing cologne and perfume. Believe it or not, poor personal hygiene is one of the fastest ways to lose a customer. And men, please make sure your ties are straight and all facial hair is neatly trimmed. The overall look to aim for is one of neatness. If you need help, pick up a book on dressing for success or, if you're really desperate, contact an image consultant.

CASE IN POINT

Most people feel more comfortable when they deal with someone who presents a neat and clean appearance. If you're sloppy, people may assume your work is sloppy as well. An advertising sales person recently failed to gain my account because his briefcase was so disorganized he couldn't find the brochures he wanted me to see. I lost respect for him as he fumbled around looking for them. I told him to forget it. If you are trying to make a deal, the person you are dealing with must have respect for you. Even if you are not out on a business call, looking good makes you feel good, helping lift your mood and your outlook on life.

LESSON

If you want to be successful, you've got to dress the part. Dress for success!

<u>Tip #24</u>

Always look your best when you're out in public.

DON'T Become a Cheap Employee at Your Own Business

"Few rich men own their own property. The property owns them."
Robert Green Ingersoll

If you start work in your business at six in the morning and work until midnight day after day, you could well calculate your earnings at less than five dollars an hour—that makes you a "cheap employee" in your own business. You might even say the business owns you. Don't let yourself get caught in this situation. Always remember that you are in business to make money, lots of money, not to sacrifice your life. Your job is to *manage* the business so it will grow while making money and having fun. Concentrate on those objectives and only on those. If you find yourself spending time doing all the little things that need to be done, like fixing the drill or the copiers, you're becoming a cheap employee. Hire people to do the little stuff.

CASE IN POINT

I've seen it happen time and again: The business owner who becomes a "cheap employee" fails within the first five years. Don't let this happen to you. Here's why it could if you become a "cheap employee."

1) Your business will own you.
2) Your family life will suffer.
3) Your social life will suffer.
4) Your health may suffer.
5) You will no longer be well rounded.
6) You will suffer burnout.
7) You will lose interest in your business.

LESSON

Maintain your perspective. Save your energy for the most important and creative tasks in your business.

Tip #25

Manage your business. Don't let your business manage you!

YOU CAN USE THIS SPACE TO:

List the aspects of your business you need to take care of yourself and the tasks you can hire people to do.

DO Stay Healthy: Physically and Mentally

"The first wealth is health"
R. W. Emerson

Entrepreneurs who forget to take care of themselves are wasting their lives—yes their lives. What is the use of creating a successful business and earning a great deal of money if you aren't around to enjoy the fruits of your labor. Please don't tell me you are doing it all for your family or your kids. Business is only one part of a life, perhaps a short part of a total life. Your family and your children need you to be a whole human being, not a burnt-out robot.

CASE IN POINT

A friend of my husband's started a business. He spent all his time there; he didn't exercise, eat right or get enough rest. Just when he started to make a go of it, he ended up in the hospital. Good health will help you to stay sharp and alert, which can only enhance your ability to make better deals. So eat right, drink plenty of non-alcoholic fluids, get plenty of rest, get outside for some physical exercise, and don't forget to take your vitamins.

LESSON

Most people take better care of their cars than their health.

<u>Tip #26</u>

Do for your body what you want your body to do for you!

DON'T Hire Relatives or Close Friends

"Although prepared for martyrdom, I prefer that it be postponed."

Winston Churchill

One of the fastest ways to ruin a happy family or a close friendship is to hire a family member or a friend to work for you. In my experience, a close friend or family member will learn to resent you for telling them what to do; they'll conveniently forget that it's you who owns the company, not them. They also may expect to be treated better or to be paid more than your other employees. The other side of the coin is that you, as the employer, may find it more difficult to act impartially toward a family member or friend or may be reluctant to offer criticism if this should become necessary. All in all, it's a lose-lose situation.

CASE IN POINT

A LONG time ago I was employed at my father's company. He had a large staff, yet he constantly expected the best performance from me because I was his own flesh and blood. He worked me harder and gave me little or no praise for jobs well done. I felt like a slave. On top of that, when I got home I had to continue "being at work." Everyone needs a break. Give yourself a break; don't hire people in your family or in your circle of close friends.

LESSON

Keep your private and business life separate. Think of the separation of church and state. It's that simple.

<u>**Tip #27**</u>

Find employees through acquaintance referrals or "cold ads" only!

DO Hire People With Nice Smiles

"A smile is a curve that sets everything straight."
Phyllis Diller

Did you know that some people make a living teaching job applicants and business executives how to smile to get ahead? That's because a smile, a nice smile that shows sincerity and reaches the eyes, makes people trust you and want to do business with you. Plus a nice smile simply makes you and your customers feel good. Smiling is natural and everyone knows how to do it. It's simply a matter of remembering to use your smile as a tool of your business. A nice smile and good eye contact will win your customers' faith and keep them coming back to your business over and over. When you staff your business, make sure to hire people with good smiles, magical smiles if possible—the Disney kind of smile that will keep your customers coming back for more.

CASE IN POINT

When's the last time you bought ice cream or another of those wonderful, fattening delights that aren't really very healthy for you? Did the cashier give you a look that made you feel guilty; did he or she have a scowling face? Of course not! The cashier probably smiled that magical smile that lit up his or her eyes, a smile that made you smile in return. And what happened? You probably went back again to buy more ice cream! The smile worked, didn't it?

LESSON

A smile makes your customers feel appreciated and keeps them coming back.

Tip #28

Keep on smiling.

DO Hire Good-Looking People

"One eye sees, the other feels."
Paul Klee, Artist

Corporate America has always believed the first impression is a lasting impression. Walk into any large corporation and nine times out of ten you'll find a good-looking receptionist behind the desk. Walk into a doctor's or dentist's office and you'll probably find the same. Businesses care about their images—don't fool yourself into thinking this isn't important, regardless of how unfair or superficial it may seem to you. I'm in no way prejudiced against how people look, and my guess is you aren't either, but the reality is, in business, that's the way it is. I can't change it, and neither can you.

CASE IN POINT

I had lunch one day with a friend who works as a salesman for a large corporation. He was upset because he was not top salesman of the month. I asked him what happened. He told me his manager had hired a new good-looking saleswoman and she was making record sales. My friend is quite nice looking, but I asked him bluntly if the new salesperson was better looking than he was. He said, "That's for sure." Then I told him he needed a haircut. He got the message.

LESSON

It may not be fair, but life's not fair. Hiring unattractive people can actually hurt your business!

Tip #29

For all positions that deal directly with the public, hire attractive people!

DO Hire People Smarter Than You

"Surround yourself with only people who are going to lift you higher."

Oprah Winfrey

If you think you are the smartest or the wittiest or the most experienced person in your particular business, believe me there is someone out there who is smarter than you! If you think you are a hurricane, you are going to be beaten by a typhoon. Some executives are afraid to hire people more knowledgeable than themselves because they feel threatened by them or afraid they'll lose their jobs to them. Remember, this is your business! Hiring a smart staff that's willing to give you ideas can only help your business grow and become more profitable. The bottom line is that you make the final decisions; you might as well do it with the support of people smarter than you.

CASE IN POINT

When I was managing the entire computer operation for an international company (my young days), I always tried to hire people smarter than me. With my experience (I had more), and their knowledge to back me up, my job became easier. We learned from each other. It was a win-win situation. Just look at the President of the United States. Thank God he has smart advisors around him. Running a country is an awesome job to tackle alone. In a way, running a business can be an awesome job too.

LESSON

Surround yourself with smart people and you'll learn even more!

Tip #30

Hire people for their knowledge, then learn from it!

DO Hire Outside Sales People

"I not only use all the brains I have, but all that I can borrow."

Woodrow Wilson

If one of your business goals is to increase your customer base, then you need a sales force out there constantly knocking on the doors...knocking.... knocking.... and knocking. You and your sales force have to get out and find the business. Customers tend to have very short memories; they need to be reminded of what your business can do for them over and over again. As the owner of a business, it's your job to find ways to reach new customers and ways to keep reminding current customers that you still want and deserve their business. In my opinion, outside sale reps are the pipelines between my business and my current and future clients.

CASE IN POINT

Most likely, your business is not the only one of its kind out there. If your sales staff is not continually approaching current and potential customers, your competitor's sales reps will be, that's for sure. The result: the customer may give his or her business to one of your competitors. You can't be everywhere at once. Hire sales people to help you reach your customers.

LESSON

Out of sight, out of mind. A sales force will help keep your business in your customers' minds.

<u>Tip #31</u>

Persistence pays.

DO Offer Incentives to Boost Moral and Increase Productivity

"Getting results through people is a skill that cannot be learned in the classroom."

J. Paul Getty

Incentives are the most effective way not only to boost your employees' morale, but also to increase productivity. Increased productivity, in turn, helps you, the business owner, meet your objectives. It's surprising how much additional effort most people will put out to earn that extra dollar. I can't explain it; I just know they do it. Over the years, I've seen people work twice as hard for that little extra incentive. In the long run, the extra money you spend on incentives will more than be repaid to you in increased income.

CASE IN POINT

After we implemented a $100 to $200 bonus for each employee in the office who reached certain levels of production, we found that production increased by almost thirty-five percent! Amazing. Not everyone will work harder for bonuses, but most people will. My advice is to try it; see how it works for your business.

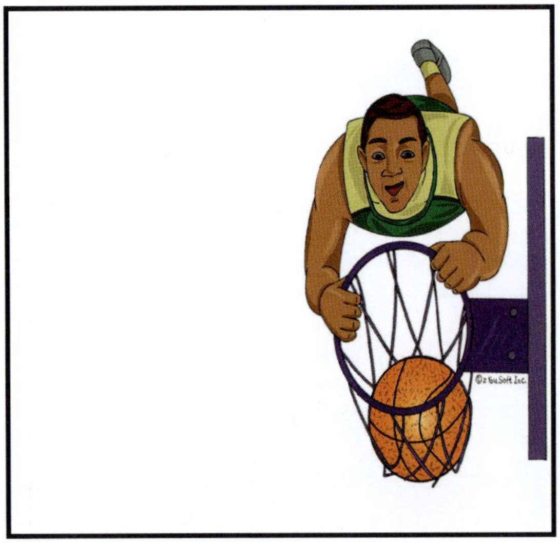

LESSON

Put a carrot in front of a rabbit and he'll exert the extra effort to obtain it.

<u>Tip #32</u>

Incentives are worth their weight in gold.
Use them!

DO Listen to Your Employees' Advice

"There are no bad soldiers, only bad officers."
Napoleon

If your company has employees, make sure you listen to what they have to say regarding the business. It is wise to have at least one scheduled meeting a week with your employees to discuss situations that have developed, discover solutions together, and give special recognition to those employees who did an excellent job the week before. People who feel they have some control over their own working conditions are happier employees and happier employees are more loyal and more productive.

CASE IN POINT

The people who work with you and for you day in and day out know your business almost as well as you do and as such can be very effective in offering solutions to problems as they arise. These people can also suggest ways to increase productivity and profits. Listening to your employees is good business. It's common sense that it's less expensive and often more effective to consult with your employees than to hire an outside consultant at a fancy price who doesn't know your business as well. That's been my experience and it's certainly worth a try. You can always hire that fancy consultant later.

LESSON

Listen, listen, LISTEN!.

<u>Tip #33</u>

Accept employees' opinions gratefully and you will get honest suggestions that truly improves your business.

DO Advertise

"No one ever went broke underestimating the taste of the American people."
H. L. Mencken

You do have a choice. You can advertise your business or you can advertise to go out of business. No matter what kind of business you are in, YOU MUST ADVERTISE. You have to let people know about your services, products, or ideas if you want to be successful. Sure, advertising can be expensive, but isn't it more expensive to lose everything you've put into the business? And remember, word of mouth is the best advertising you can have so don't ever hesitate to let people know about you or about your products and services. Shyness is not a characteristic of the successful entrepreneur.

CASE IN POINT

When I mentioned in casual conversation that my brother had a dental practice, I can't begin to count how many times I heard, "Oh? I'm looking for a new dentist!" Most of the time, I didn't have a pen to give them his number, but if I had his business card, I handed it over. I'm sure I added to his new patient list. My brother had a problem striking up conversations with strangers when he first began his dental practice. Talking about himself made him uncomfortable. It makes many people uncomfortable. But it is necessary for business owners to get over that discomfort and promote themselves and their businesses.

LESSON

Carry business cards with you at all times. Pass them out at every opportunity that comes along. You must learn to promote your business. Advertising starts with you.

<u>Tip #34</u>

The best advertising is free: Word-of-mouth!

DO Hold Sales and Annual Promotions

"The fish sees the bait, not the hook."
Chinese proverb

You won't stay in business long if you don't consistently promote your business. If you think you can avoid promoting your business, you are fooling yourself. You must never stop marketing your product or service. If you do you will be closing your doors even before that giant competitor arrives. There are many ways to successfully promote your business, but here are some rules of thumb. The conventional wisdom is to run an ad continually week after week. I agree with this advice. The purpose of the ad is to keep your business's name in the consumer's mind, a phenomenon known as "building name awareness." If you have a florist shop—say "Rosie's Roses"—you want the answer to be "Rosie's Roses" whenever someone asks if there's a florist shop in town.

In addition to the running ad, you should also plan on having one large promotion per year and up to but *no more* than four "sales" per year. These events are designed to attract new customers, especially the ones who have just moved into your area. The idea here is to grow your business and make more money.

CASE IN POINT

Let's say your business is a barbershop. Here are some ways you might advertise it. You might send out coupons three or four times a year to the residents within a five-mile radius of your shop. You might hold a "cut-a-thon" as your annual promotion. Invite local media to cover the event, ask celebrities to get hair cuts, and state in your promotional material that twenty five percent of all proceeds that day will be

donated to a charity of your choice. No, you won't make more money per haircut, but you will receive a lot of exposure and because of your charitable contribution, you will develop a good name for your business within the community. An event like this has repercussions for a long, long time!

LESSON

Make the name of your business a familiar name in your community.

Tip #35

Be creative!
Put on unusual and unique promotions
that consumers will remember!

YOU CAN USE THIS SPACE TO:

Note ideas for ways to promote your business.

DON'T Manufacture Your Product until You Sell It

"The most important word in the vocabulary of advertising is TEST. If you pretest your product with consumers, and pretest your advertising, you will do well in the marketplace."

David Ogilvy, Advertising Executive

If you have an idea for a product, service, or book...HOLD ON! Don't rush that product into production. *Sell it first.* Test the market for its reception to your product, service, or idea. Look for free ways of advertising, speak to people, remember "word of mouth." But even if testing the market costs you some time and money, it could save you a great deal of time and money in the long run. If and when you find clients who are eager to have your product, then go ahead and manufacture it. You should apply this principle whether you are an inventor with a new idea or a manufacturer with a product. Don't tie up thousands of dollars on inventory that gathers dust!

CASE IN POINT

I could have written and produced copies of this book way before I started advertising it. But I realized that I would spend considerable time and money doing so. What if it did not sell? What if no one was interested? Experience has taught me that it's imperative to find the customer for the product *before* you manufacture the product for the customer. A book or an invention is a product. I advertised this book and the response was overwhelming! I knew then, without a doubt, that this book was wanted and needed in the marketplace. I could go ahead to make the book a reality secure in the knowledge that it would sell. Best of all, the book is paying for its own production!

LESSON

Don't count your chickens before they hatch. And don't count on recouping your investment in a product until you know you can sell the product.

Tip #36

Test your market prior to production!

YOU CAN USE THIS SPACE TO:

Note ways to test the market for your product or service.

DON'T Sell Below Cost

"A man who trims himself to suit everybody will soon whittle himself away."
Charles Schwab

If you are selling a product or service, and I'm assuming you are or soon will be, you *must* know your costs. You must do the calculations to figure out exactly what it will cost you to get your product ready for the market or your service ready to implement. Your sales price for that service or product must be at least *three times* the amount of your costs! Make this one of the principles of running your business.

CASE IN POINT

Sometimes the prices your competitor's offer will tempt you to lower your prices to keep your customers. RESIST THAT TEMPTATION! Instead stress the benefits your customers receive by doing business with you rather than with your competitors. Remember, if you're going to sell at cost or below cost, you might just as well ask the customer to purchase the product from your competitor. There is no point to your making the sale. Since you won't make any money on the product, you're better off not selling it—at least you'll still have the product to sell at a price that will make you a profit. Besides, if your competitor is selling at or below their cost, they're not making any money, and no matter how many sales they make, they will soon be out of business. Then the customers will return to you because you'll still be around!

LESSON

If you are selling at cost or below cost, that's a signal that you will be out of business soon.

<u>Tip #37</u>

Price your product correctly!

DO Keep Your Eye On Expenses

"Keeping a little ahead of conditions is one of the secrets of business, the trailer seldom goes far."

Charles Schwab

Business expenses are of course an integral part of doing business. Certainly you need to spend money to make money, but be careful not to spend it faster than it's coming in. Business expenses need to be specially managed and carefully monitored. You must know what your overhead is in order to determine your profit and you don't need an accountant to tell you this. As a smart entrepreneur who keeps track of cash flow, you will know your overhead and your profit.

NOTE: See Section 22 (Paying COD)

CASE IN POINT

A business man of my acquaintance, was doing quite well with a new business he started. After a few months, the business was starting to show a profit and he began to buy expensive equipment to expand his production. But he didn't have orders or the customer base that warranted the increased expansion. Very soon his expenses far exceeded his profits. You should wait until the need is clear before you increase your expenses. I know I've said it before, but it bears saying again: Watch your money! Be careful with every dollar that goes out. You worked hard to earn those dollars, use them wisely.

LESSON

If your expenses outweigh your income for too long, find a solution. If you can't find a solution, then it's time to do something else.

Tip #38

Spend your money wisely!

DON'T Spend Your Money Lavishly

"He spends money as if he can't stand to keep anything that has anybody else's picture on it."

Jeanne Robertson, humorist

This "**Don't**" is very simple. If its meaning isn't clear to you, then you are probably not a business person. You are a kid who got lucky. Some short-term entrepreneurs succeed and quickly make a lot of money, but lose it just as fast. They often have to get out of business before their creditors catch up with them.

CASE IN POINT

The first thing I notice about fly-by-night business owners who spend their money (or someone else's money) lavishly is that they are spending it on items that are not essential to the business. They rent a very expensive, upscale office, fill it with the most expensive furniture, then hire a gorgeous and, usually, dim-witted receptionist. They are more interested in the emblems of success—an expensive car, big lunches out with clients—than in making their business grow. After a few months, they are bouncing checks. Enough said.

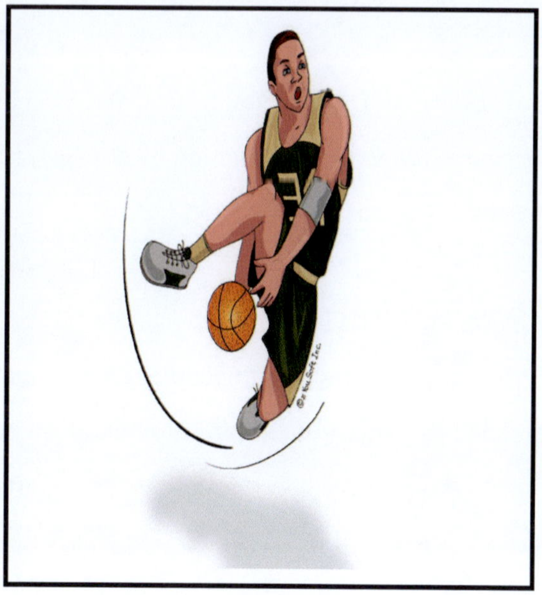

LESSON

If you're serious about being a truly successful entrepreneur, you will spend your money wisely. When you're starting out, impress people with your product or service, not your office trappings.

<u>**Tip #39**</u>

If you don't have it, don't spend it!

DO Pay Your Taxes and Keep Good Records

"It will generally be found that men who are constantly lamenting their ill luck are only reaping the consequences of their own neglect, mismanagement and improvidence..."

Samual Smiles, Scottish Author

It is so tempting to delay paying your taxes. Unlike other creditors, the government doesn't have a collection agent calling you every thirty days to remind you about your overdue bill. So when small business owners get behind in paying bills, which bills do you think they find it easiest to put the back burner? Right—the tax bills. But this is a *big mistake*. It is essential to pay your taxes--Federal income taxes, social security taxes, payroll taxes, and in some instances, state, local, and small business taxes.

Just as important as paying your taxes, is keeping good records. The two go hand-in-hand because if you are ever audited by the IRS, it's essential to have the support documents to back up the tax forms you filed.

CASE IN POINT

When I created my first invention twenty years ago, I called the Small Business Administration and they offered to give me a free small business start-up consultation. A few days later, the advisor, a retired businessman in his sixties, came to meet with me. He told me that the best advice he could give me was to pay my taxes. He explained that other creditors I might have could be negotiated with, but when it came to the IRS, it was a different story. I took his advice. Years later, when my copy shop was a victim of the economic slump, the first thing my attorney wanted to know was if my tax bill was current. Thanks to the advisor from the Small Business Administration, it was. My attorney was relieved to hear that; he said the rest was easy! He meant easy for him from a legal standpoint; losing my business was hard on me, but trouble with the IRS would have made it worse.

LESSON

If you're not a good at keeping records, if you have difficulty filing your taxes on time, if you don't believe the nightmare the IRS can create for you, maybe you shouldn't be involved in business to begin with.

Tip #40

Don't put off paying your taxes.
Take care of this expense, FIRST!

SECTION NOTES:

"Man who waits for roast duck to fly into mouth must wait very, very long time."

Chinese proverb

THE DO'S AND DON'TS OF DEALING WITH THE CUSTOMER

DO Know Your Customers

" You win customers by quality rather than price."

Jean Ridley, retail consultant

What is your target market? Who are your customers? Who do you want to do business with? What type of people will use your product or service? You need to determine your IDEAL customer so you know who to advertise to and who you'll be dealing with. Ask yourself these questions:

- What is likely sex of the customer—male, female, or both?
- What is the age range? 12-18, 25-54, 25-39, 65+?
- What is your customer's home like—a rented apartment, a mortgaged house, a condominium?
- Where does your customer live? Local city? Nearby cities? Other states? Worldwide?
- What is your customers' median annual income? $20K, $35K, $100K, Higher?
- What is the probable marital status of your customer? Single? Married? Divorced? Widowed?
- Are there likely to be children in the household? Number? Ages?

You get the idea. There are many more questions you might ask yourself about your ideal customer. Use your imagination to come up with questions about the target customers for your business. The more you know, the more successful you'll become in determining what they want, what will satisfy them, and what will keep them coming back to you again and again for business.

CASE IN POINT

What's the use of advertising in a national magazine if your most likely customers are in your own town or city? Before you can plan where, when, and how best to advertise, you need to determine where your customers are, what your customers expect, what not to offer them as well as what to offer them. How else can you get the most for your advertising dollar? How else can you know how to please your customers and encourage them to do business with you?

LESSON

Know who your customers are and what they like and dislike.

Tip #40

Get to know your customers!

YOU CAN USE THIS SPACE TO:

List questions that will help you define your target market.

DO Flatter Your Customers

"Give the lady what she wants."
Marshall Field

Here's a fact of life when you are in business: From time to time you'll have to deal with unpleasant people for the sake of making a sale. You ARE going to be nice to them. You ARE going to treat them as if they are the most important people on Earth. Why? Because you want to win them over, get their business and have them refer their friends and acquaintances to you. If you alienate potential customers, you are cutting off your nose to spite your face. It's that simple.

CASE IN POINT

You have to think of your customers as your boss, because in a sense, that's what they are. They dictate your total sales, which, in turn, determine your profits. Like it or not, to succeed as an entrepreneur, you must (to put it bluntly) do some sucking up. It may be the most unpleasant side of doing business, but you can't escape it. You have to be nice to all of your customers all of the time no matter what. Keep your eye on the prize: Closing the deal. Close many deals and you'll see your profits rise, your business grow, and your happy customers tell others about you. That will be your satisfaction. Most of the time you'll probably like your customers, but in the long run, it's worth it to pretend to like even the ones you don't really like.

LESSON

Treat others as you would want to be treated. It's good business.

Tip #41

Pucker up!

DO Listen, Listen, Listen

"Advice is seldom welcome. Those who need it most, like it least"

Samuel Johnson

Just as you should listen to your employees' ideas and suggestions, you should listen to your customers as well. I cannot say it enough: Listen! I envy the people who have a natural ability to listen.. They are *really* able to hear their customers' needs, comments, and complaints and respond to them as part of their business practices. I try to develop this quality in myself. It can only make my business more profitable. Listen to your vendors as well. Always listen first, then negotiate.

CASE IN POINT

My grade school teachers tried to teach me to be a better listener. I bet yours did the same. But my teachers never told me how I could make more money if I learned to really listen. So, I didn't listen. Throughout my years in business, I've increasingly realized that listening carefully results in increased success and profits. Now, I listen to my customers, my employees, and my vendors all the time. I even listen to my spouse, but that I learned the hard way!

LESSON

Open your ears and mind to all the information people share with you.

<u>Tip #42</u>

Listing is an art. Cultivate It.

DO Know What Your Customers Expect

"The public is like a piano. You just have to know what keys to poke."

Al Capp

All customers expect one thing: 100 percent satisfaction. Regardless of the type of business you are in, this is true of your customers and , if you want to succeed, you must never forget it. If you receive something from a mail-order catalog and you were expecting more, that catalogue is doomed. It is for this reason that photographs are so useful in advertising and presentations--they help customers know what to expect of the product so they will be satisfied when they purchase it. Although you had an idea of what this manual would be like from the sample page you reviewed before purchasing it, I hope it is not only everything you expected, but more than you expected.

CASE IN POINT

The automakers of America during the 1970's thought that if they let a lemon roll off the assembly line it was somehow okay because customers were accustomed to getting lemons once in awhile. However, the Japanese were waiting and watching and learning Through their superior quality control, they gave American customers more than they had learned to expect when they bought a car. The Japanese gave them good service, quality products every time, and satisfaction guarantees. As you know, the big three American automakers found themselves in serious trouble.

Think about what you'd expect if you bought the service or product your business offers. What is the absolute minimum that would give you 100 percent satisfaction? What extras would please and surprise you?

LESSON

Deliver what your customers expect...or more!

Tip #43

Know what your customers want and give it to them!

YOU CAN USE THIS SPACE TO:

Describe the minimum you must give your customers so they will feel 100 percent satisfied with your product or service.

DO Make Customer Satisfaction Your Number One Priority

"A business that makes nothing but money is a poor business."
Henry Ford

The customer is always 1000 percent right! If you want to increase sales and build and maintain a reputation for excellence, your business must guarantee customer satisfaction by offering to refund money for a product if the customer is not satisfied with it. Such a policy *always* works to make people feel more comfortable about their purchase. Moreover, most people are willing to pay more for the peace of mind of knowing that they can return a product they aren't satisfied with. So do account for that in your pricing. Another benefit of a liberal return policy is that your satisfied customer will tell their friends about your business, and their friends will tell their friends, and so on. This is word of mouth advertising—and it's free.

Unfortunately, there are always some people out there who will abuse guarantees, but the increase in sales that will result from this policy is truly significant and, in my opinion, makes such a policy *a must* for a successful business. Satisfied customers are the lifeblood of a successful business. Without them, there is no work, no business, no profits!

CASE IN POINT

Although *Nordstrom* (a retail department store) is expensive, I shop there regularly because their return policy makes me feel comfortable. If I don't like what I've bought when I get it home, or if I find something wrong with it, I know I can exchange it or get my money back with no questions asked. I'm willing to pay extra for this peace of mind. As a result, I always shop at *Nordstrom* when I need an item they carry. (I also

shop at *Kmart* because it too offers guaranteed refunds, although not without asking questions.) When a customer shopping for an item or a service understands that there is NO chance of being ripped off, he or she will make a quicker buying decision.

LESSON

Keep the customers happy and they'll keep coming back for more. Moreover, satisfied customers will recommend your business to their friends.

.

Tip #44

Guarantee to deliver what you promise!

YOU CAN USE THIS SPACE TO:

List ways your business or service can guarantee customer satisfaction.

DO Deliver More Than Customers Expect

"Don't bunt. Aim out of the ballpark.

David Ogilvy, Advertising Executive

This is not a new philosophy. When you give people more than they expect, even if it's just a little more, you win them over. As an entrepreneur, exceeding your customers' expectations should be one of your prime objectives. Whether you offer a service or product, this objective is something you will definitely benefit from. The customer will feel as if he or she has gotten a great deal and you will feel as if you are not just in business to make money, but to truly please the people who buy your products or services. Another win-win situation that is simply good business.

CASE IN POINT

The cobbler who fixes the broken heal for the "mean lady," then polishes the shoes for her as well, at no additional charge, has just won her loyalty. She expected the repair, but not the shine, and she is unlikely to forget it.

Lesson

Go the extra mile for your customers. Little extras make big differences in customer satisfaction and your profits.

Tip #45

**Customers are ALWAYS the most important element of your business.
Keep them happy!**

DO Deliver On-Time Service

"I have learned to use the word "impossible" with the greatest caution."
Wernher VonBraun

On-time service is another important element of customer satisfaction. Whether you deliver goods or perform a service, you must *deliver by the date you promised.* Every time you break that promise, NO MATTER WHAT YOUR EXCUSE, you lose your customer's respect and, possibly, his or her business! Don't ever use the "flat tire" excuse or any other excuse, for that matter. As a businessperson, you are supposed to prepare for potential delivery problems by having alternatives and back-ups. On-time service demonstrates to your customers that your business is a professional, well-planned operation that runs like a well-oiled machine. On-time service produces repeat customers.

If your operation can't meet the promised date to your customer, you need to make a full evaluation of the situation, then adjust accordingly. You must let the customer know *before* the promised date if it won't be met and advise of the new promised date. NEVER wait for the customer to come pick up the order and find out it's not ready!

CASE IN POINT

I bought my husband a gold watch for Father's Day. I bought it from a jeweler we'd given our business to for years, purchasing gifts and personal items for ourselves. Unfortunately, the watch didn't work. My husband returned it and the jeweler informed him he'd order another one. He asked my husband to come pick it up in two weeks. Because my husband is a very patient person, he agreed to the wait. In two weeks he returned to the store only to be told by the jeweler

that it hadn't come in yet. The jeweler then promised my husband he'd have it within a week, but he didn't. Not only that, the jeweler never called our home. My husband had to phone him to find out if the watch had arrived! Do you think we ever did business with this jeweler again? Of course not. He lost our business forever. Not very smart of him because I am very fond of gold jewelry.

LESSON

Know how long it will take you to deliver goods or services before you tell the customer a date of delivery.

Tip #46

Don't make promises you can't keep.

DO Aim for Quick Service

"If you think you can, you can. And if you think you can't, you're right."
Mary Kay Ash, Mary Kay Cosmetics

Quick turn-around is another very important objective of business and a crucial way to achieve customer satisfaction. If you haven't heard the expression before—*turn around* refers to the time it takes you to deliver the product or service after you receive the order. As I discussed in an earlier section, the business that provides more than the customer expects will be the most likely to succeed. Providing quick turn-around without sacrificing quality is one of the ways to give the customer more than he or she expects. Whether you are in the fast food business, car repair, or publication business, if you give your customer a "promised by" date (or time), and then have the order or service completed sooner, your customer will be thrilled!

Note: See Section 45 (More than Customers Expect)

CASE IN POINT

Most people in the United States live in the fast lane. They want something "now, and yesterday would actually have been better." However, some things just can't be done as fast as you or your customers would like. *Quality is always more important than speed.* How many times have you found yourself in a dentist's chair thinking to yourself "I wish he'd hurry up"? The point is, the dentist can't hurry up. If he is to do the job you expect, he needs to take his time and do it right. Do you want to have to go to the dentist again because the filling fell out or the cap came off? Think about the most realistic and reasonable amount of time it will take to deliver a quality product before you make a promise.

LESSON

Give your customers a "promised by" date that gives you more than enough time to produce quality work. This gives you the opportunity to deliver sooner, thrilling your customer!

Tip #47

Be quick, but don't sacrifice quality!

YOU CAN USE THIS SPACE TO:

List ways your business can give customers more than they expect.

DO Accept Checks

"If you're going to be a leader, you've got to take chances."
Ronnie Milsap, Country Singer

Have you ever entered an establishment where the first thing you saw was a sign reading, "Sorry, NO Checks"? Even if you didn't intend to pay by check, did that sign make you feel welcome? Such a sign will not win customers! It may even offend some customers or drive them away. People who plan on paying for their purchase by check may decide it's easier to go elsewhere than to try to find an ATM machine. Don't be afraid to accept checks because of the loss you *may* incur. If you calculate the risk correctly, the percentage of loss due to bounced checks can be included in the cost of doing business, exactly as you do for credit card charges.

CASE IN POINT

One day I was so angry that a fifty dollar check a customer gave me bounced, I asked one of my employees to post a "Sorry, NO Checks" sign. Two weeks later, a customer who owns the swimming pool supply shop across the street walked in and suggested to me that my sign was a big mistake. When I explained about the bounced check, he told me he accepted checks, didn't even ask for driver's licenses, and rarely got a check that bounced. I replied that if his customers needed pool supplies, they must be rich! He said that was not the issue; the issue was one of trust and calculating the cost of keeping good, honest customers. He was 100 percent right!

LESSON

Learn to trust your customers and your business will reap the rewards.

<u>Tip #48</u>

Trust your customers and they'll be back!

DO Accept Credit Cards

"Education is a wonderful thing. If you couldn't sign your name you'd have to pay cash."
Rita Mae Brown, Playwright

Entrepreneurs MUST accept credit cards. Yes, there is a small fee to the business, but the advantages far outweigh the disadvantages. America is a country built on debt. The average American doesn't even carry cash anymore; he or she carries plastic because is replaceable if lost, convenient, and enables the consumer to keep a record of expenses. I would like to emphasize that you should, in my opinion, even accept *American Express*. Many companies do not accept *American Express* because it costs more for them to do so or because *American Express* did not authorize them for one reason or another. If you are authorized to accept *American Express,* do it. It creates a stronger image of your company in the eyes of the other businesses you deal with.

CASE IN POINT

I find that people who carry credit cards, especially *American Express* tend to spend more money, so I never hesitate to accept all major credit cards and I don't think you should either. You never know when that high roller will come in carrying only a credit card. Do you really want to say to that customer, "Sorry, I don't accept *American Express* (or whatever)," then watch as he or she walks to your competitor's to make the purchase? I don't think so.

LESSON

People spend more with credit cards than with checks or cash. Don't give them the opportunity to walk out. Accept all the credit cards you can get authorization to accept!

<u>Tip #49</u>

Let your customers charge away!

DO Keep Your Eye on Your Money

"The meek shall inherit the earth but not the mineral rights."

J.Paul Getty

Most customers will pay for their purchases with cash, credit cards, or checks. However, if the majority of your sales are to other businesses, you may find it necessary to bill your clients on a monthly basis. Hello headache and hassle! First of all, check credit references on the business before you open up their account. And stay on top of the money you are owed. This money is known as A*ccount Receivables* or AR. You need to have a set procedure on how to collect Account Receivables. Such a procedure might be a monthly bill, followed by a telephone call, followed by a collection company. The point is you must have a system in place for your Account Receivables because you MUST keep your eye on your money! Don't let your collections get behind.

CASE IN POINT

The longer it takes people or businesses to pay you, the better the odds are of not collecting the money at all!

Lesson

Keep track of your money. COLLECT MONEY OWED TO YOU AS SOON AS POSSIBLE!

Tip #50

Set up a collection system and stick to it.

DON'T Extend Credit To Small Customers

"If you're not in the parade, you watch the parade—that's life."

Mike Ditka

When I say small customers, I don't mean little people or children. I'm referring to customers who don't spend much money on your product or service. No matter what kind of business you are in, you will have customers who want to open an account so they can walk in at anytime and charge their purchases from you. There is nothing wrong with this IF the customer meets the qualifications you've established in advance. You must set minimum as well as maximum spending guidelines. A minimum guideline is the minimum amount you expect a customer to spend every month in order to qualify for a charge account at your business. If you don't have minimum guidelines, it's too easy for those customers to fail to pay you or simply to disappear.

CASE IN POINT

In my copy center, I had a customer who came in about twice a month to make copies. Foolishly, I approved his charge account because he told me he would give me a lot of business in the future and I believed him. My staff bent over backwards to make him a satisfied customer. However, he continued to charge approximately $30 a month. It cost me more than $30 to do his monthly billing! One day he just disappeared. It was not worth extending credit to this customer.

LESSON

When customers who spend only small amounts of money for your product or service want to open an account, advise them you will gladly accept their credit cards. If they don't have a credit card....be tough and say <u>no</u>. You are in business to make money, not give charity.

<u>Tip #51</u>

Set account guidelines and don't make exceptions!

SECTION NOTES:

"The dawn does not come twice to awaken a man."

Arabic Proverb

THE DO'S AND DON'TS OF DETERMINING IF IT'S TIME TO SELL

DON'T Be Afraid of Goliath

"A superior man is the one who is free from fear and anxieties."

Confucius

The ideal entrepreneur, like David , is young and smart. It doesn't matter what your chronological age is if you are young in your heart and it doesn't matter what your IQ is if you are smart about the way you conduct your business. Figure out what can set you apart from everyone else in a similar business. This difference between you and your competitors is your niche in the marketplace. To find your niche you must study the competition carefully, including Goliath. *Visit Goliath. Study Goliath.* Ask yourself the following questions:

- What does "Goliath" have and what kind of service does it provide?
- Where are <u>your</u> prices compared to Goliath's?
- If your prices are higher, does your service compensate for them?
- What product or service could YOU specialize in that will set you apart from Goliath?
- What can you do to keep your customers loyal to you?

Remember, service is an asset you can count on.

CASE IN POINT

Does Goliath deliver merchandise to its customers' homes or businesses? Is delivery a service your customers need that you can offer? Does Goliath offer a low-fat alternative on its menu? Do your customers want that? If you think Goliath is coming to your town, you have to plan how you will compete with it. You may feel like running out of town, but that would be taking the chicken's way out. Instead, decide upon your niche, focus directly on it, advertise it, and remember, David got the best of Goliath.

LESSON

If you've got it (a niche), flaunt it!

Tip #52

Find a niche that makes you indispensable to your customers.

YOU CAN USE THIS SPACE TO:

Make notes on what you can offer your customers that Goliath can't.

DO Plan for Goliath

"Only a strong tree can stand alone."

Arnold Glasow

When a big shark eats a small one, it's a natural part of life. This is nature: the food chain, the survival of the fittest. I can't feel sorry for the small bookstore owner who was very successful until the day *Barnes and Noble* (Goliath) opened up next door and began stealing his customers. The owner of the small bookstore had neglected to plan ahead, to plan for expansion while retaining customers. If you are planning to start a business that has a giant competitor out there, you need to be aware of this big shark...because he will come. You need to be prepared for him, you need to figure out what you can offer your customers that he can't, and you need to start fighting him before he even arrives!

CASE IN POINT

In general, customer loyalty is a thing of the past. Customers are very fickle these days and their loyalty, if it exists at all, is very short lived....unless you do something about it!. What can you do? You can go the extra mile for your customers. You can offer them great service, a great product, a satisfaction guarantee. Think about your own loyalty to the independent businesses you still deal with. List them on the next page. Write down what makes you go to them instead of to the Goliath competitor. Planning for Goliath takes great effort, but if you don't plan for him, when he moves in next door with lower prices, you will lose your customers and be forced to close up shop.

LESSON

Keep on keeping your customers happy. What matters is the service they get from you.

Tip #53

Go the extra mile for your customers!

YOU CAN USE THIS SPACE TO:

Note independent businesses you deal with. For each, list reasons you go to them instead of to Goliath.

DO Know When to Fold

"No mistake or failure is as bad as to stop and not try again."

John Wanamaker

"The Gambler," sung by Kenny Rogers, is a great song, but, more importantly, it holds a message every entrepreneur should take to heart: Know when to fold and walk away. Every entrepreneur should sing this song once in awhile. Every time you attempt to make money on your own, you are in business for yourself . You are an entrepreneur and you are to be congratulated for being a risk taker. But just as smart is knowing when to fold.

CASE IN POINT

Entrepreneurs tend to love what they're doing. They become so emotionally involved they sometimes can't see the big picture anymore; they can't simply let go when the time is right. I've heard entrepreneurs say that running a business is like nurturing a child. Although it may seem like it at times, this is not true. Your love and loyalty for a child is absolute and permanent. A business is NOT a child. Don't forget that. Don't underestimate the value of the advice in this final section of the manual.

LESSON

There's a time to walk away from a business in order to keep your profits and reduce your losses.

Tip #54

Everything has its season.
Know when it's time to close up shop!

DO Sell When You Get an Offer

"When ya come to a fork in the road—take it."
Yogi Berra

When I say sell, I mean sell. If you think you are too young to sell or too old to start over, neither are true. Don't let your age stop you. If you get an offer to sell your business, DO IT. You'll be amazed at the opportunities that will open up to you after you sell that did not exist or you did not pay attention to before because you were so involved in building and keeping your business. Sell and enjoy!

CASE IN POINT

As an entrepreneur, you get your biggest joy from starting something and watching it grow. I know I do. When your business is grown, it's time to sell and move on to bigger and better things!

Lesson

Keep joy in your life. For an entrepreneur, joy comes through exploring the unknown by creating and growing new businesses. You can't do that when you're involved in a mature business.

Tip #55

If you receive a reasonable offer, sell!

NOTES:

SUMMARY
OF THE
DO'S AND DON'TS
OF
DOING BUSINESS

THE DO'S AND DON'TS OF DOING BUSINESS

The Start-Up

Do think big!
Do be positive
Don't associate with negative people
Do get into a business you'll like and enjoy
Don't get into a business you know nothing about
Don't start from scratch
Do buy an established business
Don't buy a business that's in the red
Don't join a franchise
Don't choose a retail business if you don't like dealing with people
Do believe in your product
Do have a short-term plan
Do have a long-term plan
Do secure your idea
Do incorporate
Don't invest your own money
Don't borrow from relatives
Do obtain working capital
Don't buy expensive equipment
Don't buy used merchandise from people you don't trust
Don't sign expensive leases
Don't sign long-term leases
Do pay COD when you start
Do create a strong color logo

Conducting Business

Do pay attention to your appearance
Don't become a cheap employee
Don't let the business own you
Do stay healthy: physically and mentally
Don't hire relatives
Don't hire close friends
Do hire people with nice smiles
Do hire good-looking people
Do hire people smarter than you
Do hire outside sales people
Do give incentives to boost moral
Do listen to your employees' advice
Do advertise
Do hold sales and annual promotions

THE DO'S AND DON'TS OF DOING BUSINESS (cont.)

Conducting Business (cont.)

Don't manufacture your product until you sell it
Don't sell below cost
Do keep your eye on expenses
Don't spend your money lavishly

The Customer

Do know your customer (target market)
Do flatter your customers
Do listen, listen, listen
Do know what your customers expect
Do make customer satisfaction your number one priority
Do deliver more than customers expect
Do deliver on-time service
Do aim for quick service
Do accept checks
Do accept credit cards
Do follow your money
Don't extend credit to small customers

Time to Sell?

Don't be afraid of Goliath
Do plan for Goliath
Do know when to fold
Do sell when you get an offer

SUGGESTIONS / COMMENTS

As one entrepreneur to another, I welcome your suggestions and comments about this manual. If you have any personal stories you'd like to share, or ideas for subjects not covered in this manual that you believe should be, please write them below and mail to:

SHS
13790 Rosecroft Way
San Diego, CA 92130

Printed in Dunstable, United Kingdom

91222436R00056